PRAYERS FROM THE NICU

USER WARNING

THE CONTENTS OF THIS BOOK ARE EMPHATICALLY INTENDED TO DEPOPULATE THE NICU THROUGH RESURRECTION POWER ONE PRAYER AT A TIME

By: Shameika Brown

Scripture quotations, if any, are taken from the Holy Bible.

Printed in the United States of America

Published by: Shameika Brown Ministries

ISBN: 978-8-234-06560-5

For permissions, contact: info@shameikabrown.org

For My Children

To my children, Wyncelin and Justin-

your lives are my greatest testimony of God’s grace, strength, and sustaining power. Everything I endured was worth it because of you.

Acknowledgements

To my husband **Ajani**, thank you for your unwavering love, strength, and covering. Thank you for never leaving my side, and for never leaving our son's side. Your faith in God and your steady presence carried us through some of the hardest moments of our lives.

To my son **Justin**, you are one of the greatest gifts of my life. Thank you for your strength, your patience, and your love for your brother during this journey.

To my parents, **Walter & Sandra Snipes**; thank you for your love, support, and foundation. **Mom**, thank you for teaching me how to be a mother when I had my oldest son, Justin. *I miss you* more than words can express. Kiss my baby girl in heaven for me. **I love you** dearly. **Dad**, thank you for always being present, always steady, and always there when I needed you most. I love you so much.

To my sister **ShaKeya**, my best friend and the godmother of my children; thank you for standing with me, praying with me, and carrying me when I felt like I could not carry myself.

To my in-laws, **Kenneth & Sue-Etta Brown**; thank you for your presence, especially in the hospital when Wyncelin was born and during the most painful moments when I lost Twin A. Your love and support meant more than words can express.

To my brother and sister-in-law, **Walter Lee & Tanya Snipes**; thank you for your love, consistency, and support throughout this journey.

To my spiritual parents, **Apostle Chris & Prophetess Haley Johnson**; thank you for your prayers, your love, your encouragement, your support, the phone calls, the gifts, and spiritual counseling that you gave throughout this journey.

To my writing coach, **Jerrica Brumfield**; thank you for your wisdom, guidance, patience, and belief in this message. You helped give structure to a story that carried so much weight.

To **Glory Culture Church**, thank you for your prayers, love, covering, and community. You stood with us in faith when we needed it most.

And finally, to my son **Wyncelin**, my miracle. You are the evidence that God restores, heals, and redeems. You came into my life not only as my child, but as part of God's healing in my heart after loss, grief, and transition. Your life is a testimony that God still speaks, still heals, and still performs miracles.

And thank You **God** for every breath, every moment, and every miracle in this story.

TABLE OF CONTENTS

Chapter One

The Neurological System

When the Brain Is Still Being Formed

Whether you are believing for a baby in the NICU, a loved one in hospice, a family member facing neurological decline, stroke recovery, or cognitive uncertainty, you are not reading this as an outsider. You are invited into this moment. Insert the name of your loved one, or your own name where applicable. These prayers are meant to be spoken aloud and personalized.

When my water broke at **22 weeks** and **six days**, everything shifted in an instant.

What followed was **31 days** of hospitalization, **twenty-seven** of those days my son lived without **amniotic fluid**. No cushion. No protection. No medical explanation that could fully account for how he was still alive. The only thing sustaining him was God's hand and the **umbilical cord** delivering nutrients, moment by moment.

The doctors were clear and compassionate, but also honest. Without **amniotic fluid**, there were real and serious risks. They warned us about the possibility of **brain bleeding** or multiple **bleeds.** They prepared us for concerns about his **vision**. They explained how the lack of **fluid** could affect his ability to **breathe** and that **oxygen** deprivation could impact **neurological** development.

I received **steroid** shots. I received the **magnesium**. We did everything medically possible. And still, the tone remained the same: ***We do not know if it will be enough***.

When Wyncelin was born, he weighed **two pounds**, **1.2 ounces**, tiny, fragile, and fierce all at once. Almost immediately, the medical interventions began. A **brain** cap was placed on his head. An **eye** patch covered his eyes. These were not decorations; they were safeguards monitoring for **bleeding**, protecting developing systems, and watching closely for what could go wrong.

And yet, standing beside that incubator, my husband and I made a decision. We would not let fear have the loudest voice in the room.

Every day, we prayed. Not timid prayers. Not vague hopes. We spoke directly over his **brain**, his **nervous system**, his **eyes**, and his development. We decreed these words over his incubator, declaring that his **neurological** system would form and function according to the design of God, not the predictions of statistics.

Within days, the scans came back. No **brain bleeds**. Within two weeks, the **eye** patch came off. What medicine monitored God preserved.

Prayers & Decrees for the Neurological System

The following section contains the prayers and declarations spoken daily over Wyncelin's neurological development. These are written as they were prayed intentionally, boldly, and with expectation.

Prayer for Brain Function and Protection

We decree that Wyncelin's brain will function properly and perfectly, exactly as You designed it to.

We rebuke every form of head bleed, hemorrhage, or neurological injury now. There will be no damage, no delay, and no dysfunction in Jesus' name.

We speak directly to the brain and command it to come into divine alignment. We speak to every structure, every system, and every function, and we declare order where there could have been disorder.

Prayer Over the Brain Structures

We speak to the cerebellum and decree proper coordination, balance, and development.

We speak to the brainstem and command it to regulate breathing, heart rate, and vital functions with precision and stability.

We speak to every lobe of the brain, frontal, parietal, temporal, and occipital.

We decree full development and flawless communication throughout the nervous system.

Every cell will respond to the Word of the Lord.

Rebuking Premature Diagnoses

We rebuke every premature diagnosis, every negative prognosis, and every word spoken out of fear or limitation. No label, no statistics, and no medical forecast will define Wyncelin's future.

We cancel every assignment of delay, disability, or impairment now, in the name of Jesus.

Prayer for Intelligence and Capacity

We decree and declare that Wyncelin will be smart, educated, articulate, and wise. His mind will be sharp. His understanding will be strong. He will excel and thrive in every season of life.

His brain will not merely survive, it will flourish.

Prayer for Vision and Eye Development

We speak to Wyncelin's eyes now and we decree 20/20 vision with no deficiencies.

We rebuke blindness, impairment, and underdevelopment. We command every blood vessel in his eyes to form properly and fall perfectly into place.

Optic nerves, respond to the Word of the Lord. Retinas, develop in strength and clarity.

There will be no vision loss, only vision restored and perfected.

Declaration of Completion

We declare that what God started in Wyncelin's neurological system, He will complete. His brain will grow, mature, and function in divine timing and divine order.

We seal these prayers in faith and with the blood of Yeshua, believing not just for survival but for wholeness. In Jesus name. Amen.

These prayers are not limited to the NICU. They are language for anyone believing in God for restoration, protection, and divine alignment in the mind and nervous system at any age, in any season

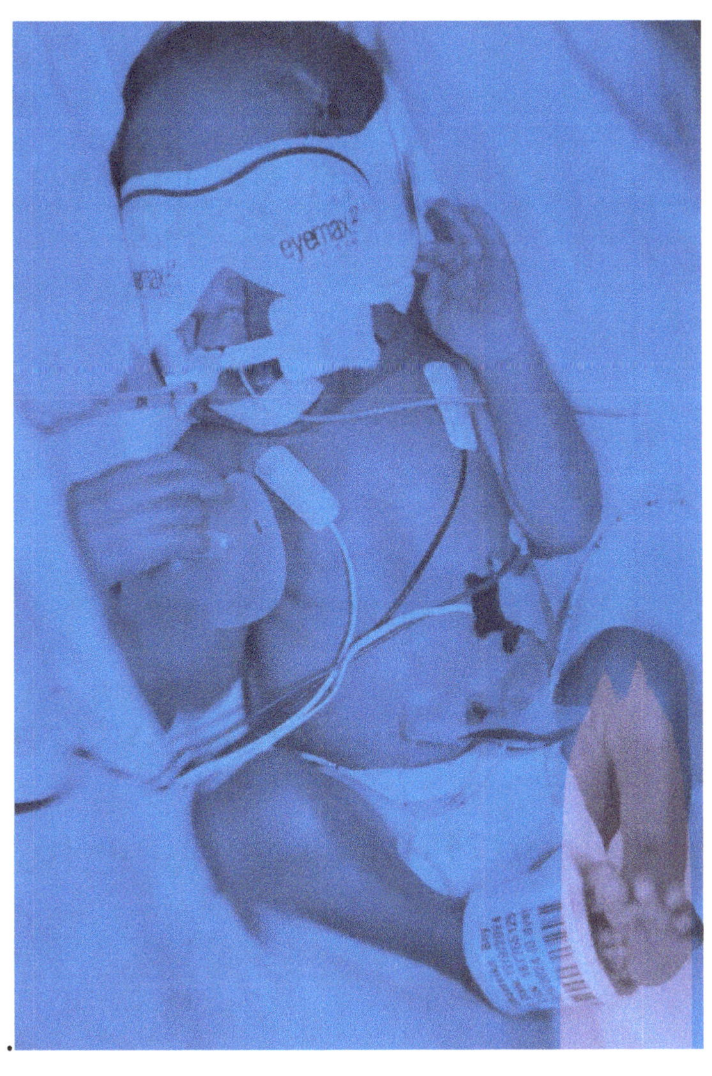

Wyncelin wearing protective eye bands during phototherapy treatment.

Chapter Two

The Cardiovascular System

When the Heart Must Learn to Beat on Its Own

As you read, insert the name of your loved one or your own name where applicable. These prayers are meant to be spoken aloud and personalized.

When a **baby** is born extremely early, their **heart** is doing something it was never meant to do alone.

In the **womb**, a mother's **body** assists in regulating **heart rate** and rhythm. Thc **amniotic fluid**, the warmth, and the natural environment help carry the load. But when that environment is suddenly gone, a premature **baby's** heart must learn very quickly how to function independently.

This is where **bradycardia**, often called **"brady episodes,"** comes in.

Wyncelin experienced **brady** episodes early on. His **heart rate** would suddenly drop, and the nurses would rush to **stimulate** him so it could rise again. At times, these episodes happened multiple times a week. Because of his size and **gestational** age, the medical team placed him on **caffeine,** a common **NICU** intervention used to help regulate **heart rate**.

We were grateful for the tool, but we believed God was the source.

So, while the monitors beeped and the numbers fluctuated, we stood at his incubator and decreed something higher.

We declared that Wyncelin's **heart** would learn its rhythm. We declared that he would not have to depend on **caffeine** long-term. We declared that God Himself would stabilize his **heart** steadily, safely, and completely.

There were moments that tested our faith. Twice, Wyncelin required immediate intervention because his heart took longer than expected to recover. But even in those moments, God kept him.

Within about a month, Wyncelin no longer needed **caffeine.** He required no **heart surgery**, no long-term **cardiac intervention**, only time, prayer, and divine alignment.

What follows are the prayers and decrees we spoke daily over Wyncelin's heart.

Cardiovascular Decrees and Prayers

The following section contains the prayers and declarations spoken daily over Wyncelin's cardiovascular development. These are written as they were prayed intentionally, boldly, and with expectation.

Prayer for Heart Function and Rhythm

Father God, in the name of Jesus, we place Wyncelin's heart in Your hands. We decree that his heart will function properly, efficiently, and fully according to divine design.

We speak to every chamber, every valve, and every vessel, and we command them to work together in perfect unity.

Declaration Against Bradycardia

We rebuke bradycardia now. Heart rate, you will not drop unexpectedly. You will not falter. You will not fail.

We decree that Wyncelin's heart will always maintain a stable and healthy rhythm.

Declaration of Sinus Rhythm

We decree and declare that Wyncelin's heart will remain in sinus rhythm. There will be no irregularity, no instability, and no disorder in the electrical pathways of his heart.

Every signal will fire correctly. Every beat will be strong.

Breaking Dependence on Caffeine

We declare that Wyncelin will not depend on caffeine or man-made substances to regulate his heart. God, You are his regulator. As his heart matures, it will strengthen naturally and respond to Your perfect timing.

Prayer for Continued Formation and Stability

Father, continue forming and stabilizing Wyncelin's heart. Let growth be steady. Let development be complete. Let nothing rush ahead of its time and let nothing lag.

We decree that his cardiovascular system will support his body fully, without strain or struggle.

Declaration of Preservation

Even in moments of delay or recovery, we declare preservation. Wyncelin's heart will respond. His body will recover. His life will be sustained.

We seal these prayers with faith and the blood of Yeshua, believing that Wyncelin's heart will not merely survive but thrive.

In Jesus name. Amen.

These prayers are not limited to the NICU. They are language for anyone believing in God for restoration, protection, and divine alignment in the cardiovascular system—at any age, in any season.

Chapter Three

The Respiratory System

When the Lungs Must Learn to Breathe

As you read, insert the name of your loved one or your own name where applicable. These prayers are meant to be spoken aloud and personalized.

When Wyncelin was born on **December 9, 2024**, the first sound we heard was his cry. That cry mattered. It told us he had **lungs** but having **lungs** and having functioning lungs are two vastly different things, especially for a **baby** born this early.

While I was still in the operating room, my husband followed Wyncelin down to the **NICU**. That is when the medical team pulled him aside and spoke plainly.

"Mr. Brown," they said, ***"we don't want to say we're scared but we aren't going to say we aren't concerned."*** Wyncelin was sitting at **100%** supportive **oxygen**. His **lungs** were fragile, immature, and doing everything they could just to keep up. The expectation was that **respiratory** support would be long-term.

My husband stood there with his *tallit* in his hand while hearing the medical team say our son was **extremely** sick. Ajani responded with faith that he refused to bow to fear.

"I hear what you're saying, and I know medically you are supposed to tell me this," he told them, ***"But we will not use those words to describe him. I serve a God who can do exceedingly and abundantly above all we could ever ask or imagine."***

Then he prayed for something bold. ***"God, You have 24 hours to turn this around."***

Within 24 hours, Wyncelin was no longer on **100%** oxygen.

The medical team came back to us and said, ***"We do not know what happened, but your son is doing better. And we really believe this is going to be a good moment for him moving forward."***

That was only the beginning.

When Wyncelin was born, he was **intubated**, and we were told he would remain intubated for quite some time. But within four days, Wyncelin **extubated** *(he took his breathing tube out)* all by himself.

He never went back. From that moment forward, we prayed not just for survival but for **maturation**, strength, and divine order in his **lungs.**

Respiratory Decrees and Prayers

The following section contains the prayers and declarations spoken daily over Wyncelin's respiratory development. These are written as they were prayed intentionally, boldly, and with expectation.

Prayer for Breath and Stability

Father God, in the name of Jesus, we thank You for the breath of life in our son. We decree that Wyncelin's respiratory rate will be normalized and stable.

We rebuke tachypnea now. Rapid, labored breathing will not have authority over his body.

Prayer for Lung Development

We speak directly to Wyncelin's lungs. Lungs, you will develop fully. You will mature properly. You will strengthen daily.

We decree that every alveoli will form correctly, every airway will open, and every breath will move freely in and out.

Declaration of the Ruach of God

We decree that the Ruach of God, the breath of God blows on Wyncelin daily. As God breathed life into Adam, He breathes life into Wyncelin now.

He will not stop breathing. He will not struggle for breath.

Declaration of Expansion and Function

We decree that Wyncelin's lungs will expand, inhale, and exhale with strength and consistency.

No collapse. No restriction. No regression.

Breaking Dependence on Machines

We decree that Wyncelin will breathe on his own without machines, without assistance, and without limitation.

Man-made support served its purpose, but God completes the work.

His breathing will come steadily, in divine timing, and in a way that supports healthy growth in Jesus' name.

Declaration of Completion

What God has begun in Wyncelin's lungs, He will finish. We seal these prayers with faith and the blood of Yeshua, believing that Wyncelin's respiratory system is in full alignment with the backing of the Holy Spirit.

In Jesus name. Amen.

These prayers are not limited to the NICU. They are language for anyone believing in God for restoration, protection, and divine alignment in the respiratory system, at any age, in any season.

Chapter Four

Hematologic, Homeostasis, & Sepsis Evaluation

Blood, Balance, and the Threat of Infection

As you read, insert the name of your loved one or your own name where applicable. These prayers are meant to be spoken aloud and personalized.

December 23, 2024.

It was supposed to be a normal day, at least as normal as life could be with a baby in the **NICU**. My husband, my oldest son, and I were out to eat, making plans to go Christmas shopping and then see *Mufasa*. For a moment, life felt almost ordinary.

Every Monday, Wyncelin had **labs** drawn because I work in the medical field, checking **MyChart** had become part of my routine. Not out of fear, out of responsibility. I logged in casually, scrolling with practiced **eyes,** when one number stopped me cold.

His **pH** was low.

Immediately, my mind went where experience takes it. Low **pH** meant **acidity. Acidosis**. A system under strain. I looked at my husband and said quietly, reflexively, "Wyncelin's **pH** dropped, I just pray he's not becoming **acidic.**"

Before the sentence could even settle, my phone rang.

It was the **NICU**.

It was the **Nurse Practitioner**. She began explaining Wyncelin's lab results, and I told her, ***"I had already seen them."*** Then the conversation shifted from observation to intervention. She explained that they were concerned about **infection** and wanted to proceed with a **lumbar puncture**.

A **lumbar puncture** is a long needle into one's **spine** and Wyncelin had just reached **twenty-eight** weeks.

She carefully walked us through the risks, the complications, and the protocol. I could hear her words, but my spirit was already somewhere else. Right there at that restaurant table, I bowed my head and began to pray.

I called every value into alignment. **Alkaline phosphatase**. **Creatinine. Hemoglobin**. **Hematocrit.**

I rebuked **anemia** aloud. I spoke life over his **PO_2 capillary levels,** his **phosphorus,** his **chloride**. I declared balance where numbers suggested instability. Order where the report hinted at chaos.

I told the Nurse Practitioner plainly, ***"I hear what you are saying. But do not do anything until I get to that hospital."***

And they waited.

When I arrived at the **NICU**, I gave my consent for the **lumbar puncture**. As they prepared him, I spoke directly to the Lord. ***"He will come through this simply fine. There will be no infection. I do not care what the numbers say. You are the Chief Physician."***

They started Wyncelin on **antibiotics** as a precaution. **IVs. Needles.** Tiny arms bearing more than they should ever have to carry. I stood at his incubator and wept watching my days-old son endure what no mother ever wants to witness.

Within **twenty-four** hours, the labs began to return. **No infection**.

They monitored him for **three** days. Ha! I was reminded by heaven that Jesus was also dead for **three** days, but he got up. Every single day, the same report: **no infection**. His **blood** began to regulate. Balance was restored.

The care team looked at me and said, ***"This is good, no infection Mrs. Brown."***

I looked back at them and said, ***"God is good."***

Decrees & Prayers Over Wyncelin's Blood and Internal Balance

The following section contains the prayers and declarations spoken daily over Wyncelin's hematologic development. These are written as they were prayed intentionally, boldly, and with expectation.

Commanding Blood Stability and pH Balance

We pray and decree that Wyncelin's pH would stabilize and return to normal, declaring balance over his blood and body in Jesus' name.

We decree that his alkaline phosphatase would regulate, and that every number on his blood panel would trend toward normalcy now, according to the order of heaven.

We decree and declare that his creatinine would regulate, normalize, and reflect healthy kidney function.

We speak directly to Wyncelin's hemoglobin, decreeing that it would properly produce red blood cells and align perfectly with his blood supply and growing body.

We decree that his hematocrit would be stable and normalized, reflecting strength, oxygenation, and life.

Rebuking Anemia, Acidosis, and Internal Imbalance

We rebuke anemia, declaring that our son would not lack iron, strength, or vitality.

We rebuke all acidosis; we speak to his kidneys and declare that the Spirit of God would away wash every acidic imbalance.

We rebuke all infirmity, disease, and infection, declaring that sickness has no legal right to remain in Wyncelin's body.

We reminded heaven and we reminded ourselves that by Jesus' stripes, we are healed, and that we do not have to bear sickness because Christ already bore it on the cross.

Decreeing Healthy Oxygenation and Cellular Function

We speak directly to Wyncelin's PO_2 capillary levels, calling them into full alignment and proper oxygenation.

We decree that phosphorus levels would come down and stabilize, aligning with healthy metabolic function.

We decree that chloride levels would come down and remain normal, establishing internal balance and peace within his body.

Declaration of Completion

Every prayer was spoken with faith. Every decree was released with authority, and every lab result eventually testified that God is faithful.

We decreed these prayers and trusted that they were already answered in Jesus name, Amen.

These prayers are not limited to the NICU. They are a language for anyone believing God for restoration, protection, and divine alignment in the blood, internal balance, and immune system, at any age, in any season.

Chapter Five

Dermatology

Jaundice, Light, and the God Who Regulates the Skin

As you read, insert the name of your loved one or your own name where applicable. These prayers are meant to be spoken aloud and personalized.

When Wyncelin was born at **26 weeks** and **5 days**, one of the first visible challenges we faced was **jaundice**. His skin showed signs of **bilirubin** buildup, and the medical team placed him under **phototherapy**, the blue light treatment used to help the body break down excess **bilirubin**.

He was so **small**, so fragile, and so new to the world, and yet already under constant **medical** care. Every day, he laid beneath the glow of those blue lights wearing protective **eye** shields to protect his developing **vision**.

I remember the nurses explaining that **jaundice** in premature **babies** can take time to resolve. They said, ***"This may take a while before the levels come down."*** But in my spirit, I could not accept **delay** over my son.

And I said, ***"Not my boy Jesus, we don't receive that."***

Every day, my husband and I prayed over his **skin**. We prayed for God to **regulate** his body, to restore **balance**, and to allow his **liver** and systems to function in alignment with life. We spoke life over his **skin**, his **organs**, and his ability to process what his **body** needed to release.

We believed that even under the blue light, God was working a greater light within him and within less than **10 days**, something shifted. The levels began to normalize, and Wyncelin no longer needed

phototherapy treatment for **jaundice.** The light that once covered him was removed.

What was expected to take longer became a short testimony of restoration. I remember his team saying, ***"Mrs. Brown we have more good news. Wyncelin's bilirubin levels are normal. His jaundice is gone."*** Jesus did that **ALL** by himself. What the **NICU** said could take a long time. God did it in **HALF** the time. What can God **NOT** do? **NOTHING**! He is the Chief Physician!

Decrees and Prayers We Spoke Daily

The following section contains the prayers and declarations spoken daily over Wyncelin's dermatology development. These are written as they were prayed intentionally, boldly, and with expectation.

Regulation of Bilirubin and Internal Balance

We decree that Wyncelin's body would regulate bilirubin naturally and efficiently.

We command his liver and systems to function in divine alignment and order.

Restoration of Skin Pigmentation and External Signs of Healing

We speak to his skin and declare healthy pigmentation and restoration now.

We pray that no organ in his body will lag development or function.

We declare that jaundice would not linger and would not return.

Divine Order Over the Epidermis and Developing Systems

We ask you Lord to release divine order into his epidermis and every developing system.

We declare that even under phototherapy, God you are the true healer working behind every light.

We rebuke prolonged jaundice and any delay in healing.

Acceleration Into Wholeness and Completion

And we declare that Wyncelin would come out from under the blue light in God's perfect timing expedited, complete, and whole. We seal these prayers in the name of Yeshua. Amen

These prayers are not limited to the NICU. They are language for anyone believing in God for restoration, protection, and divine alignment in the integumentary system at any age, in any season.

Chapter 6

Gastrointestinal System

Feeding, Growth, and the God Who Sustains

As you read, insert the name of your loved one or your own name where applicable. These prayers are meant to be spoken aloud and personalized.

When it came to Wyncelin's **gastrointestinal system**, one of the biggest focuses in the **NICU** was not just survival but growth.

In **premature babies**, feeding is not automatic. Their **digestive systems** are still developing, their coordination between sucking, **swallowing**, and **breathing** is still forming, and every **milliliter** of **nutrition** matters.

Incredibly early on, I also faced the reality of my own **body** not producing a strong **milk** supply. Because he was **born** so early, my milk production was limited, and I found myself pumping constantly throughout the day, healing, praying, and trying to collect enough milk to bring to the hospital.

For about the first month and a half of his **NICU** stay, I was able to provide breast milk consistently. That became one of my daily assignments; pumping, labeling, transporting, and bringing it to him as often as I could.

After that season, his **nutrition** transitioned more heavily to formula, and his feeding plan became even more structured and monitored. At that stage, he also had a **feeding tube** to support him, ensuring he received what his body needed while he continued developing the ability to feed on his own.

We began to pray intentionally over his **stomach** and **digestive system**. We prayed that God would calm any sensitivity in his **belly**, that his body would tolerate feeds well, and that anything not aligned with life and growth would be burned out by the fire of God.

We specifically prayed that he would not require long-term feeding support, that he would not need a **GI tube**, and that his **bod**y would learn to **eat**, **digest**, and thrive naturally.

And the medical reality was sobering. We were told that **babies** born early, especially with my complications and his lack of **amniotic fluid** for 27 days often require **feeding tubes** for six months or longer. That expectation felt heavy, but it did not change what we believed.

We stood in faith for something different.

We prayed that he would transition from **tube feeding** to bottle feeding at the right time. We declared that he would learn to suck, swallow, and breathe in alignment with healthy development. We asked God to accelerate what naturally takes time.

And then, something shifted.

As he approached the **60-to-90-day** mark, his **feeding tube** was removed. He began taking bottles. Slowly at first, then more consistently, and then confidently. And once he made that transition, he never went back.

No regression. No reversal. Just progress. What had been described as **long-term dependency** became a short chapter in his journey.

God had the final say over his **nourishment**, his growth, and his ability to receive life.

And through it all, I learned something deeply personal: God was not only sustaining his **breath** and **heartbeat**, but He was also teaching his **body** how to receive provision.

Decrees and Prayers Over the Gastrointestinal System

The following section contains the prayers and declarations spoken daily over Wyncelin's gastrointestinal development. These are written as they were prayed intentionally, boldly, and with expectation.

Commanding Digestive Strength and Function

We decree that Wyncelin's digestive system will function in perfect alignment with God's design. Every organ involved in digestion will mature, strengthen, and operate efficiently.

We speak life over his stomach, intestines, liver, and all supporting systems, and we command them to receive, process, and utilize nourishment properly.

Rebuking Feeding Intolerance and GI Complications

We decree that feeding will not be a struggle but a strengthening process.

We command every feeding intolerance, complication, or delay in digestion to cease now in Jesus' name.

We declare that his stomach will be at peace, no sensitivity, no inflammation, no distress.

Declaring Growth, Weight Gain, and Developmental Progress

We decree healthy weight gain, steady growth, and consistent development over his body.

We speak to his metabolism and declare balance, order, and efficiency.

We rebuke failure to thrive, malabsorption, and any disorder that would hinder his growth.

Breaking Dependency on Feeding Tubes and Medical Support

We declare that he will not need long-term feeding tubes or GI intervention, but will learn to feed, digest, and thrive on his own.

And we speak that every ounce he gains is evidence of God's sustaining power.

We seal these decrees in faith, believing that the same God who gave him breath and heartbeat is also the God who sustains his growth.

In Yeshua's name. Amen.

These prayers are not limited to the NICU. They are a language for anyone believing God for restoration, protection, and divine alignment in the digestive system, growth, and nourishment at any age, in any season.

Chapter 7

The Day He Got Dressed

One Of My Favorite Memories in the NICU

As you read, I pray you look for a moment where God reminds you that HE is continuing to work it out for your good.

January 14, 2025. Oh, what a wonderful day that was.

"Mrs. Brown…"

The NICU nurse's voice came through the phone, calm but smiling, I could hear it.

"Wynnie is moving to clothes." In the **NICU** everyone called him Wynnie.

I did not even respond. I just froze. Then I dropped the phone.

Tears filled my **eyes** before I could even catch my **breath**, and all I could say was, ***"Thank You, Jesus… Thank You for Your goodness and Your mercy."*** Because unless you have lived in the **NICU**, you do not understand what that moment means.

Clothes are not just clothes.

Clothes mean progress.

Clothes mean **growth.**

Clothes mean your **baby** is strong enough to come out from under the lights, out of just a diaper, and step into something that looks a little more… normal.

Clothes meant more than warmth.

Clothes meant identity.

And as I sat there looking at my son dressed for the first time, I could not help but think about **Joseph** in the **Bible.**

When Joseph's father **(Jacob)** placed that robe on him, it was not just a garment. It was a sign. A declaration. A visible representation that he had been set apart, marked, and chosen for something specific. The robe distinguished him. It separated him. It spoke before he ever said a word.

And as I looked at Wyncelin in those tiny clothes, I felt that same revelation settle in my spirit. This was not just a **NICU** milestone. This was a sign that God had kept him, covered him, and was continuing to set him apart for a purpose that could not be interrupted even by **premature birth**, even by **medical** uncertainty, even by the odds stacked against him.

Clothes meant he was transitioning.

Clothes meant he was coming out of one **level of care** and into another.

Clothes meant that what once required **intense intervention** was now stabilizing.

It was natural at that moment, but it was also deeply spiritual.

For weeks, Wyncelin had been in that **incubator** with just a diaper, wires, monitors, under the warmth of those lights. Every ounce of his care was intentional, measured, and watched. And now… he was ready.

I remember when the nurse sent me the picture. My baby. Dressed. He looked like the most precious little doll I had ever seen. So tiny, but so strong. I stared at that picture repeatedly, taking in every detail like it was the first time I was really seeing him.

This was a high moment for us. One of those moments that reminds you: God is moving, even here.

Behold, I am doing a new thing; now it springs forth, do you not perceive it? I will make a way in the wilderness and rivers in the desert". Isaiah 43:19 ESV

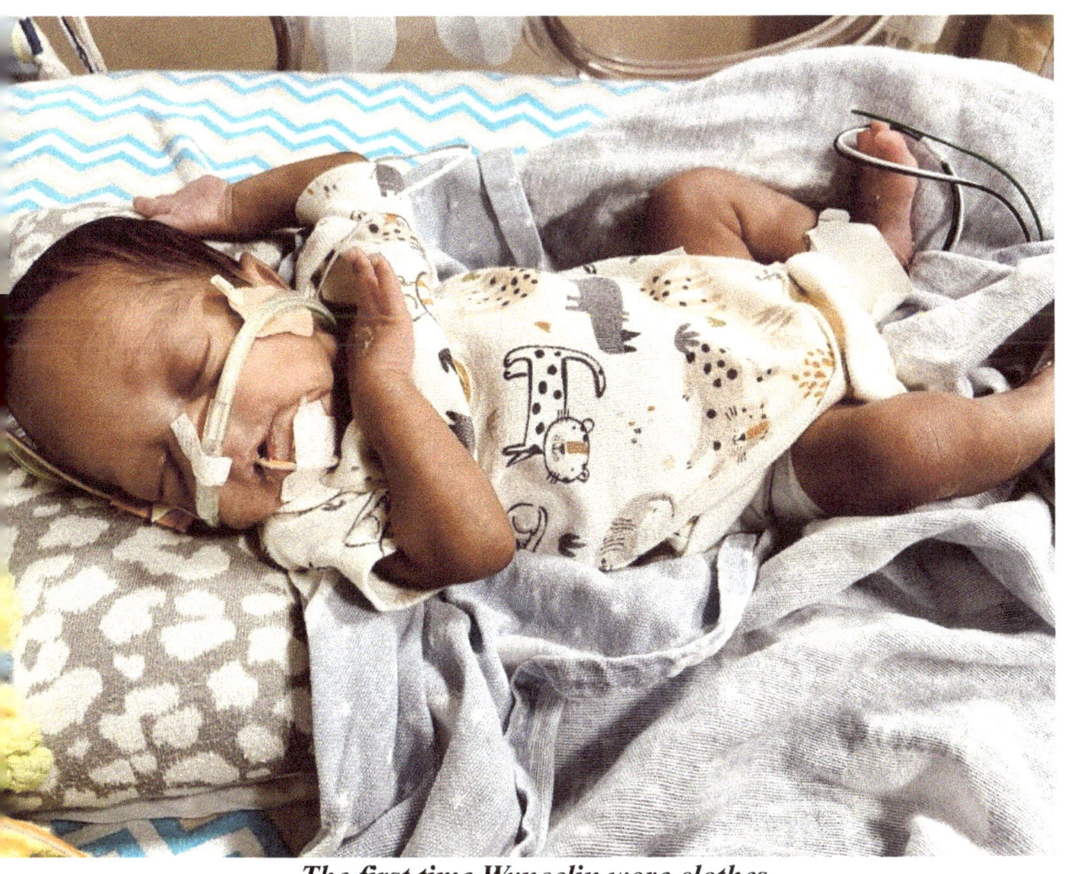

The first time Wyncelin wore clothes

Chapter 8

Infection Scare #2, Inflammation, and Protection

Skin Largest Organ in the Body

As you read, insert the name of your loved one or your own name where applicable. These prayers are meant to be spoken aloud and personalized.

During this season, Wyncelin had begun to make encouraging progress. He was **breathing** well on **nasal cannula oxygen** and showing signs of stability that brought us so much hope.

But a few days after his first round of **shots**, we noticed changes. He started having a few **bradycardia** episodes, and his **lab** results came back abnormal. That moment immediately shifted the atmosphere in the **NICU**.

The medical team responded quickly and placed an **IV** in his arm and foot to begin treatment. They explained their concern that there could be an infection present, and they warned us again that in premature infants, **infection** can escalate quickly and potentially lead to **sepsis.**

They immediately started him on **antibiotics** as a precaution, but I remember sitting there and saying, ***"I rebuke that. He does not have sepsis."***

Soon after, tests confirmed that he did have a **staph infection**. The doctors continued **antibiotics** for another week and explained that **staph infections** in premature babies can sometimes spread to the **bones** or **bloodstream** if not controlled.

But again, we stood in prayer and faith. We declared that this **infection** would not spread. We commanded it to remain contained and to leave his **body** completely.

We prayed over every **IV line**, every **lab result**, and every **report.**

And the **staph infection** stayed stationary. It did not spread to his **blood**. It did not reach his **bones**. It did not advance beyond what it was.

Within days, Wyncelin was weaned off **IV antibiotics**, and the lines were removed. His body responded to treatment, and stability returned.

What was feared to become severe, became contained, controlled, and resolved. All because our language never changed.

Before we prayed, we understood what we were confronting. **Staph** is a **bacterial infection** that can spread through the **skin,** enter the **bloodstream,** and in premature infants, potentially travel to the **bones** or **vital systems** if not contained.

But even with that knowledge, we decided: We would not let fear interpret the **diagnosis**. We would let faith respond to it.

Decrees and Prayers Over the Largest Organ in the Body

The following section contains the prayers and declarations spoken daily over Wyncelin's skin and integumentary development. These are written as they were prayed intentionally, boldly, and with expectation.

We rebuke all infirmity, disease, and infection now.

We declare that no sickness has the authority to overtake Wyncelin's body.

We speak directly to this staph infection, and we command it to die at the root, now in Jesus' name.

You will not grow. You will not multiply. You will not spread. You will not survive.

Commanding Containment

We decree that this infection will remain stationary.

It will not travel through his bloodstream. It will not reach his bones. It will not spread to any organ or system. We command full containment now.

Every bacterial cell, be restricted, halted, and be eliminated.

Prayers Over the Skin

We speak to Wyncelin's skin, the largest organ in his body.

Skin, you will function as a protective barrier exactly as God designed.

You will resist infection. You will not break down under pressure. You will heal, regenerate, and restore.

We decree that no bacteria will be able to penetrate or overtake what God has established.

Protection Over Bones and Internal Systems

We specifically cover his bones now.

We decree that no infection will enter, settle, or spread within his skeletal system.

Bones, you are protected. Bones, you are covered. Bones, you will not carry infection.

We declare that every internal system is shielded and preserved by the blood of Jesus.

Authority Over Inflammation and Response

We speak to every inflammatory response in his body. Inflammation, you will not escalate beyond what is necessary.

You will come into divine balance now. No excessive swelling. No systemic reaction. Only what is needed for healing and nothing more.

Declaration of Healing and Resolution

We decree that Wyncelin's body will respond to treatment swiftly and completely.

Every antibiotic will function with precision and effectiveness. His immune system will recognize, respond, and recover.

We declare full healing, no residue, no recurrence, no regression.

We seal these prayers in faith, declaring that what was meant to spread will be stopped. What was meant to escalate will be contained. And what was meant for harm will be turned into a testimony.

In Yeshua's name. Amen.

These prayers go beyond the NICU. They are a language of faith for anyone standing in belief for restoration, protection, and divine alignment in the integumentary system at any age, in any season, and in every circumstance

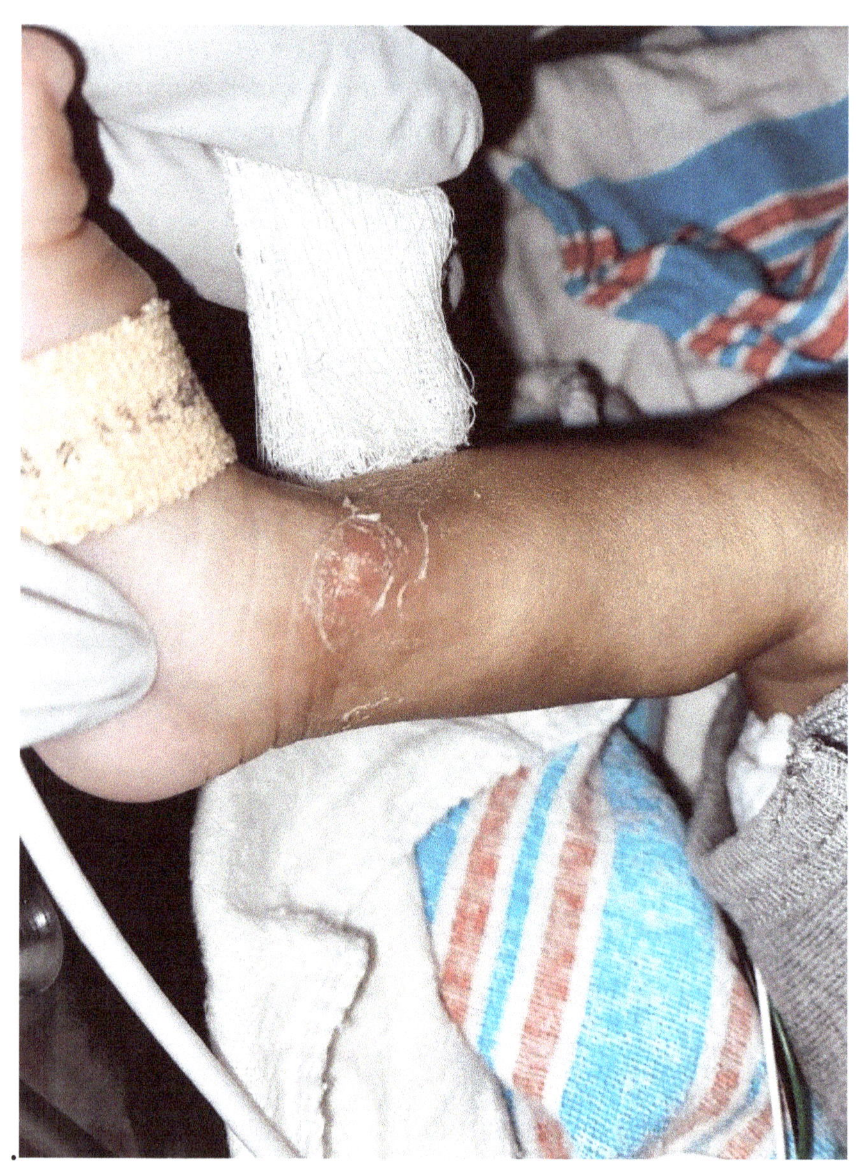

Here is the Staph Infection on Wyncelin's Foot

Chapter Nine:

Boom Boom Comes Home

The God Who Delays for Protection

As you read this chapter, I pray you remember that sometimes delay is not denial; it is divine protection.

The God Who Delays for Protection

Boom-Boom is Wyncelin's Nickname.

Wyncelin's original due date was **March 12, 2025.**

That date became a quiet anchor in our hearts. We believed that by March 12th, he would be home. Fully healed. Fully stable. Fully done with the **NICU** journey. That was our expectation. But heaven had a different timeline.

As we got closer to discharge, Wyncelin had a **small procedure**. After that procedure, he required a **blood transfusion** and that moment shifted everything.

What looked like a step forward turned into a brief step back. His **body** needed time to recover, **stabilize**, and respond. And just like that… discharge was delayed. Not denied but delayed. Those days stretched our faith in a unique way because when you are this close to "home," every extra day feels like a mountain.

In that space, I remember praying something simple but honest: ***"Lord, let his body regulate quickly. Let this transfusion do exactly what it needs to do. Let there be no complications, no reactions, and no impurities in his blood."***

I believed for a two-day turnaround but then I heard the Lord gently correct my expectation, not in fear, but in peace: ***"It is not time yet, Shameika. My delay is his protection."***

And then He reminded me: ***"You asked for him to come home with no oxygen. You asked for him to come home whole."*** And I realized something in that moment, God was not late. He was being intentional.

Those final days were not wasted days. They were completion days. Days where God was making sure: every system was **stable**, every number was aligned, every **risk** was closed, every fear was finished and then, on **March 27, 2025**, it happened.

Wyncelin was **discharged**. **No oxygen**. **No medical equipment**. **No monitors. No long-term support systems.**

Just life. Just breath. Just wholeness. A **baby** born at **26 weeks** and **5 days.** A mother whose water broke at **22 weeks** and **6 days**. A child who lived **27 days** without **amniotic fluid**. A **NICU** journey that lasted **109 days**. And yet, he came home. Not halfway healed. Not partially dependent but **whole.**

We were told the journey could take **six** months to a year, but God wrote a different outcome. Three months, that is all it took for what looked impossible to become testimony.

And I need you to hear this clearly: Do not let anyone, not statistics, not timelines, not **medical predictions** define what God can do in your situation.

God always has the final say.

Decrees & Prayers for the Final Stretch

The following section contains the prayers and declarations spoken daily over Wyncelin's metabolic development. These are written as they were prayed intentionally, boldly, and with expectation.

Divine Protection Over Blood Transfusions

We decree that every blood product given to Wyncelin would be pure, compatible, and fully aligned with his body's needs.

We declare no rejection, no contamination, and no adverse reaction in Jesus' name.

Rapid Regulation and Stabilization

We speak to his body and command immediate stabilization.

We decree that every system would respond quickly, efficiently, and in divine order.

No Complications from Medical Intervention

We cancel every assignment of complication, delay, or regression from procedures or treatments.

His body will not spiral backward; it will move forward.

Complete Restoration and Readiness for Discharge

We decree that Wyncelin's body would reach full readiness for discharge.

No lingering issues. No unresolved concerns. No hidden instability.

Acceleration Into Wholeness

We declare acceleration over every remaining process.

What should take time will be completed in divine speed and divine order.

Declaration of Completion

We seal this chapter with thanksgiving that Wyncelin did not just survive the NICU, he graduated from it whole. We declare what God started, He finished.

In Yeshua's name. Amen.

These prayers go beyond the NICU. They are a language of faith for anyone standing in belief for restoration, protection, and divine alignment in the integumentary system, at any age, in any season, and in every circumstance.

Chapter 10

Twin A

This Chapter is for my Daughter

My prayer is that this chapter reminds you that NOTHING is impossible with Jesus Christ.

The Life We Held, The Life We Released, and The Life We Fought For.

A Promise in the Middle of Grief

In the summer of 2024, I found out I was **pregnant.**

Just months after losing my mother on **February 9, 2024**, this pregnancy felt like God wrapping healing around my grief. It felt like **restoration**. It felt like hope returning.

We were on vacation at *Disney World* when I noticed slight spotting. I remember feeling nervous but, in the shower, I heard the Lord clearly: ***"Shameika, do not worry. There are twins."*** And when we got home, the ultrasound confirmed exactly what God had spoken.

Two **babies. Twin A** and **Twin B**. Each with their own **sac**. Each with their own **placenta**. Each with their own space. They were **Di-Di Twins.**

A Dream Fulfilled

I had always wanted **twins**. Since I was a little girl, I dreamed of it, prayed for it, imagined it.

And now here they were, alive and growing beautiful. Every **ultrasound** felt like a promise.

The Day Everything Shifted

On September 5, 2024, something felt off. That morning, I felt light… airy… not like myself.

My sister took me to my appointment, and when we saw the **babies,** they were perfect.

For the first time, they had found each other. Lying next to one another… as if they were holding each other.

The Night That Changed Everything

That night, the **pain** came. **Sharp. Deep**. Unignorable. I told my husband, ***"Something is not right."*** But before we could even leave…I stood up and my **water** broke. **Fluid. Blood**. Everything at once. I was going into **labor.**

I ran to the bathroom crying out: ***"Lord, You are not going to let anything happen to my children."*** We rushed to the hospital.

The Loss

In the emergency room, they examined me and then came the words no mother is prepared to hear early: **"Mrs. Brown… you are in labor."**

At that moment, everything inside of me wanted to collapse. But something in me said: ***"Be strong."*** Right there… I gave birth to **Twin A**. My daughter.

The Miracle

And then, God moved. After delivering her, my **cervix** closed. It sealed up and I told them, ***"Wait I am pregnant with twins."*** The doctors were stunned because that is not how this works. They brought in the **ultrasound** machine and there was **Twin B**. Alive. Strong **heartbeat**. Still fighting.

Uncharted Territory

The next day, I went to my doctor. She looked at me and said: ***"We have never seen this before." "This is uncharted territory."*** And then came the recommendation:

Terminate the pregnancy.

Go to another **state.**

Remove the **baby**.

Remove the **risk**.

I asked her to step out. I looked at my husband and said, ***"I don't want to do that."*** And in that moment, I felt compassion for every woman who has ever sat in that kind of decision.

Scared. Confused. Pressured.

But I made a choice and I chose life. Then in that moment I said to the Lord***: "If I choose life, I need You to respond."***

The Threat

The following week, I went to **Maternal Fetal Medicine**. They examined me again. **Twin B** was still there healthy, moving, and strong. But then they performed a **pelvic** exam, and everything shifted again. They found something. The **umbilical cord** of Twin A… was still inside of my **body**. They looked me in my **eyes** and said:

"This is **dangerous**."

"This will cause **infection."**

"You could develop **sepsis**."

"You and the **baby** could **die**."

And once again, they encouraged us: Go to another state. End the **pregnancy**. Remove the **cord.**

The Breaking Point

I asked them to step out and I broke. I cried out and said, ***"God… why is this happening?" "I just lost my mom. I just lost my daughter. And now they are telling me I could lose my life too? I cannot take anything else."*** But even in that moment…I chose life again. We are not going anywhere. We are going to trust God.

The Decree That Shifted Everything

When we got home, my husband placed his hand on my **stomach** and he prayed with authority:

"There will be no **infection**."

"There will be no **disease**."

"There will be no **premature death**."

"There will be no early **termination** of life."

"And this **umbilical cord**, you will come out."

The Miracle in the Shower

The very next day, I got in the shower and when I stepped out…I felt something. I looked down and there it was. The **umbilical cord**. It had fallen out.

Heaven Responded

I immediately called **Maternal Fetal Medicine**. They were in shock. At my next appointment, they confirmed it: It was gone and from that moment on, even their **language** shifted. They said they would trust my belief that this was the right decision.

Carrying Both Loss and Life

I kept going. Week after week. Appointment after appointment.

Holding grief in one hand… and faith in the other.

I told the Lord I would not fully grieve until after I gave **birth** to **Twin B.**

The Hidden Covering

But there was something else. Something I did not fully understand until later.

Twin A's placenta…never left. It stayed with me the entire pregnancy.

And on the day Wyncelin was born, in the operating room, I delivered it.

After all that time. It was as if God kept a piece of her **placenta** with me to help hold Wyncelin in place. Only God can do something like that!

What This Journey Taught Me

I wanted to share this part of my story so you would understand something: There will be moments in life you will not understand. Moments of **grief**. Moments of **sorrow.** Moments that do not make sense, but one thing will always remain: If you have a relationship with Jesus, He will come through.

A Life of Prayer

I am grateful for a **prayer** life. I am grateful to my **parents** who taught me how to pray and not give up. I am grateful for a husband who prays without **ceasing**. I am grateful for the **community** that carried me when I could not carry myself.

Because this journey required all of it.

The Final Truth

When **doctors** at one of the top hospitals in Georgia say: "***We've never seen this.***" "***It's uncharted territory.***" And God still moves… You realize something: He is the Chief Physician. There is nothing too hard for Him. Nothing **impossible**. Nothing beyond His reach.

For The One Reading This

I pray that when you read this chapter, you understand: You can **cast** your cares on Him. You do not have to **carry** the weight. You do not have to carry **fear**. You do not have to carry the outcome. Give it to Him. He will carry it for you.

Decrees & Declarations

The following section contains the prayers and declarations spoken daily over Myself. These are written as they were prayed intentionally, boldly, and with expectation.

I decree that my body aligns with the will of God.

I declare that every foreign element introduced to my body will function exactly as Heaven intended.

I decree that there will be no infection, no contamination, and no complication.

I declare divine regulation over my body, every system, every function, every response.

I decree that delays will not deny me; they will protect me.

I declare that what God has spoken over my life will happen in full.

I declare that my children will live and not die and declare the works of the Lord.

I declare that I will not come home incomplete. I will walk in total wholeness.

Call to Salvation

If you have read my story and you are wondering how I made it through, it was not strength. It was not luck. It was Jesus. There were moments I wanted to give up. Moments I did not understand. Moments where the only thing I had left… was prayer. And every single time, He met me there. The same God who carried me…the same God who preserved my son…the same God who made a way where there was none…He is available to you. You do not have to carry weight anymore. You do not have to figure it all out. You do not have to live life alone.

The Bible says that if you confess with your mouth and believe in your heart that Jesus Christ is Lord, you will be saved.

If you are ready to give your life to Him, you can pray this:

"Jesus, I give you, my life.

I surrender my fears, my pain, and my questions.

I believe that You are Lord.

I believe that You died for me and rose again.

Come into my heart.

Make me new.

Teach me how to trust You.

From this day forward, I am Yours.

In Jesus' name, Amen."

If you just prayed that prayer, heaven is rejoicing and so am I.

If this is your first time giving your life to Christ, I do not want you to walk this journey alone. I would love to walk alongside you.

Email mc at ***info@shameikabrown.org*** and let me know you said yes to Jesus. I want to pray for you, encourage you, and help you grow in your relationship with Him. You do not have to figure this out yourself; community matters, and I am here for you.

Because if there is one thing I have learned through every moment of this journey, it is that God is both a keeper and a finisher.

Even though he keeps, I remember when I saw my miracle taken from the OR…I would soon discover that my story was not over. There was another moment; one I did not see coming, where my own life would hang in the balance. In that moment I would need the same God who carried my son…to carry me.

But that…is a story for another time.

Thank you for reading, we pray this book blesses you and gives you language that hell cannot stand.

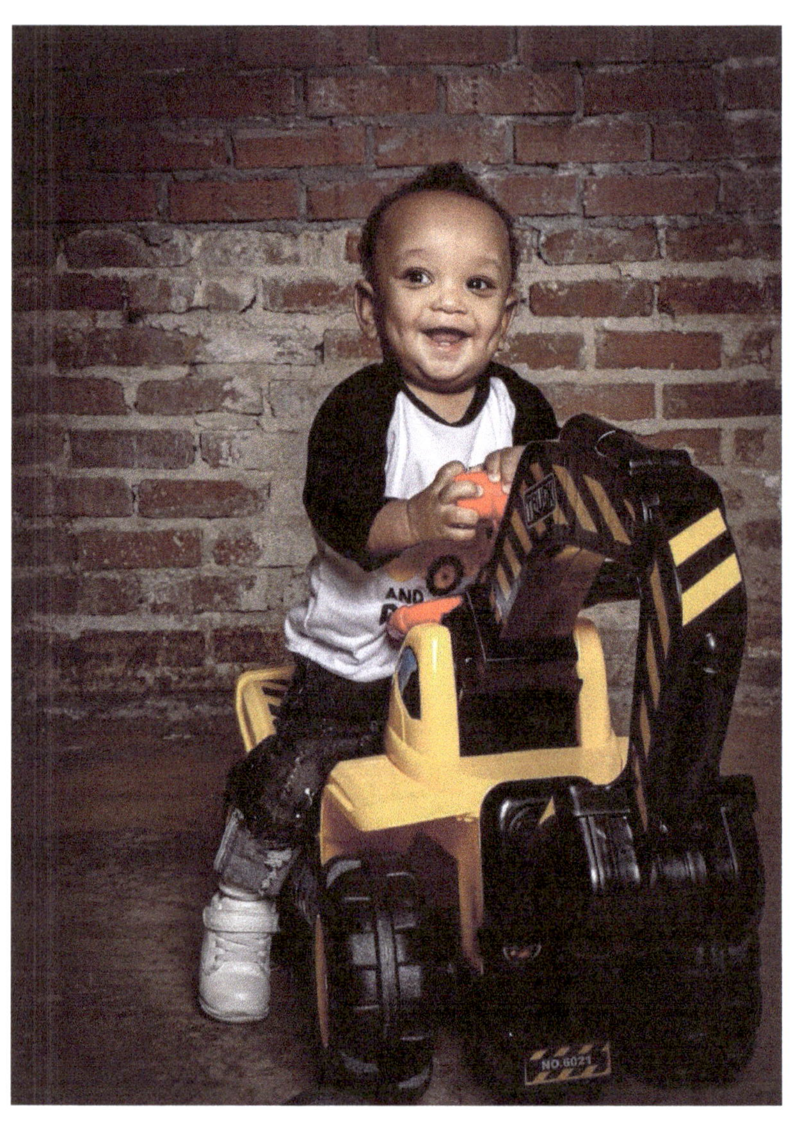

Here is Wyncelin at his first birthday photo shoot. You are looking at a miracle!

Code Blue to Breakthrough: Understanding What You Hear

Antibiotics: Medications used to fight bacterial infections.

Prayer Focus: Let healing flow through every part of the body and remove all infections.

Apnea: A temporary pause in breathing that can happen during sleep or rest.

Prayer Focus: Lord, sustain every breath and bring uninterrupted life and rhythm.

Blood Pressure (Hypertension): The force of blood moving through the body; when elevated, it can strain the heart.

Prayer Focus: Bring balance, calm, and perfect alignment to the body.

Bradycardia (Brady): A slower than normal heart rate that can affect how blood and oxygen move through the body.

Prayer Focus: Lord, bring strength, rhythm, and stability to every heartbeat.

Caffeine Therapy: A treatment used to stimulate breathing, especially in premature infants.

Prayer Focus: Awaken and strengthen every system in the body.

Desaturation (Desat): A drop in oxygen levels in the blood.

Prayer Focus: Father, let every level rise and remain stable and full.

Feeding Tube (NG Tube): A tube used to deliver nutrition directly when someone cannot eat normally.

Prayer Focus: Let every source of nourishment bring strength and growth.

Incubator: A controlled environment that helps regulate temperature and protect the body while healing.

Prayer Focus: Cover and sustain with divine protection and care.

Infection: When harmful bacteria or viruses enter the body and cause illness.

Prayer Focus: *Lord, fight on our behalf and bring complete healing and restoration.*

Inflammation: The body's response to injury or infection, often causing swelling or discomfort.

Prayer Focus: Father, bring calm, healing, and restoration to every affected area.

IV (Intravenous Therapy): A way to deliver fluids or medication directly into the bloodstream.

Prayer Focus: Let everything entering the body bring healing and no harm.

Oxygen Saturation (O2 Levels): Measures how much oxygen is being carried through the blood.

Prayer Focus: *Let every cell be filled and sustained with life-giving oxygen.*

Oxygen Support (Nasal Cannula): A device that delivers oxygen through the nose to assist breathing.

Prayer Focus: Let every breath be filled with life and ease.

Pulse Oximeter: A device that measures oxygen levels and heart rate.

Prayer Focus: Let every reading reflect healing and stability.

Reflux: When stomach contents flow back up, causing discomfort or feeding issues.

Prayer Focus: Bring peace to the body and proper function to every system.

Respiratory Support: Any treatment that helps maintain proper breathing and oxygen levels.

Prayer Focus: Strengthen the lungs and restore full function.

Stability: A state where vital signs like heart rate, breathing, and oxygen remain consistent.

Prayer Focus: Establish peace, order, and consistency in the body.

Tachypnea: Faster than normal breathing, often a sign the body is working harder to get oxygen.

Prayer Focus: *God, regulate every breath and bring peace to the body.*

Ventilator: A machine that helps a person breathe when they cannot do so fully on their own.

Prayer Focus: God, be the breath of life and restore natural strength.

Reflections

Take a moment to pause and reflect on what you've read. Let these questions guide your heart and thoughts.

1. What part of this journey impacted you the most?

   ____

2. Where have you seen God move in your life?

   ____

3. What are you believing God for right now?

   ____

4. What fears do you need to release?

   ____

5. What does healing look like for you?

   ____

6. What scripture are you holding onto in this season?

   ____

7. What has this experience taught you about faith?

____

8. Where do you need strength right now?

____

9. What are you grateful for, even in this moment?

____

10. What has God spoken to you recently?

____

Prayer Journal

This space is for you to pray, process, and pour your heart out to God.

There is no right or wrong way, just be real.

Lord, I Need You

Help Me

Dear God

Faith Declaration

Pour It Out

Time with God

Speak, Lord I'm Listening

Final Prayer

Heavenly Father,

Thank You for being the God who sees, the God who hears, and the God who heals. Thank You for walking with me through every moment, every fear, every question, every tear, and every victory.

Even when I didn't understand, You were still faithful. Even when I felt weak, You were still strong. And even in the moments where the outcome was uncertain, You remained constant.

Today, I choose to trust You.

I trust You with my body.
I trust You with my loved ones.
I trust You with every diagnosis, every report, and every unknown.

Lord, You are the ultimate healer. You are greater than any condition, any complication, and any circumstance. There is nothing too hard for You.

So I surrender it all to You.

I lay down fear.
I release anxiety.
I let go of control.

And I receive Your peace.

Fill me with faith that does not waver. Strengthen me where I feel weak. Remind me that You are near, that You are working, and that You are still performing miracles today.

No matter what I face, I will not lose hope.

I will stand on Your promises.
I will declare Your truth.
I will believe for healing, restoration, and breakthrough.

And even in the waiting, I will worship You.

Because You are good.
Because You are faithful.
Because You are God.

In Jesus' name,
Amen.

If you are reading this book from a hospital room, a waiting room, your home, or a place of exhaustion and uncertainty, this entire book is for you

www.ingramcontent.com/pod-product-compliance
Lightning Source LLC
LaVergne TN
LVHW020513100826
845148LV00003B/771

* 9 7 9 8 2 3 4 0 6 5 6 0 5 *